My DNA Search for My Roots

D1563006

Some of the names have been changed to protect identities; otherwise, these are my memoirs.

By Perline Porter

This book is dedicated to my little sis JoJo. Without JoJo's help and constant encouragement to tell my story, this book would have never been written.

Me (left) and my sis JoJo (right)

1. INTRODUCTION

My story is a tale for every person who has been adopted, illegitimate or otherwise, and is searching for his or her biological father or mother. It outlines how I conducted my search using DNA analysis. In the past some people gave up children for adoption or denied them their parentage because sometimes they wanted to ignore the responsibilities of parenthood and the shame of their mistakes (as if giving life to a precious human is a mistake). I have never believed in abortion because I always felt that I was an unwanted pregnancy, and if abortion was easily available back in the 1950s, I would not be here today.

DNA does not lie. Many studies and advancements in this science are being developed. New discoveries are being made to unlock the truth about our past. DNA can help find our ancestry; our biological families, where we came from, and our lineage can all be traced through DNA.

I struggled for many years searching for my biological father and family, and it resulted in a happy ending. It was through the new era of DNA testing advancements and

Internet sites that it was all possible. There were many disappointments, depressing periods, and times when I just wanted to give up. But stamina, persistence, and encouragement from my little sister, JoJo (Jolene Burnie), and Search Angels groups as well as many genealogists, family, and new acquaintances, I have met on my journey helped me stay on my path. It all confirms that it took a village to solve my DNA story. Anyone can solve his or her story by persisting and learning about the DNA paths.

2. MY EARLY DOUBTS

My journey started when I was a very young girl. I felt like I was different from my brothers and sisters. My family was of Hispanic descent and lower middle class, which was probably typical of the 1950s era. I was the third-oldest child, and had an older brother, James, and older sister, Sheila. We were told that we were Harry William Holbert's children. My younger siblings, Jolene (JoJo) Garcia, Randy Garcia, Debra Garcia, and Todd Garcia were all supposedly children of my stepfather, Jose A. Garcia (Joe). My stepfather, Joe, was a good man and always worked his regular job for the government at Hill Air Force Base and a second job to support us. My mother was an alcoholic, but Joe did not drink. I guess he figured Mom drank enough for the two of them. My childhood was riddled with the typical challenges of an alcoholic mother and many emotional experiences that I believe made me the strong, successful person I am today.

I estimate I was around 10 years old when I suspected something was different. My older sister and brother would tease me and say my real father was an African American man. I didn't look like my siblings. I had straight, dark-brown hair and beautiful hazel eyes that looked green or blue depending on what I wore. But was interesting was my older brother and sister didn't resemble each other either. I always felt like something was different and I wasn't the same as they were. I remember being very proud that I was Harry Holbert's daughter and would brag to my classmates. I once took a big ruby ring that was my father's for show-and-tell. My birth certificate listed Harry Holbert as my father and Mary Cisneros Holbert as my mother and said I was born on December 10, 1955, in Ogden, Utah.

3. MY MOTHER'S STORY

The story told to me by my mother was that she and her sister were given to her grandmother to be raised because after the death of her father, her mother could no longer support them. She was raised by a strict grandmother and wanted to get out of the house, so when she was of age, she married Harry W. Holbert in Las Vegas, Nevada. He owned or ran a bar and store in Cima, California, San Bernardino County. There were stories that their marriage was an arranged one and other stories that it was true love. The important factor was that Harry was about 31 years older than my mother, which made the story of it being arranged more likely. My mother's upbringing was not a pleasant one, and marrying a man 31 years older than she was proved to only add to her grief. Harry died in Kelso, California, and left my very young mother with two small children in a place where she had no family to help her. She moved back to Utah after his death and traveled back and forth between Utah and Kelso, California to take care of Harry's estate. It was confirmed in newspaper articles; found in the *Ogden Standard Examiner,* that my mother was located in Ogden in August of 1954. That would have been only four months after Harry's death and makes sense because she would have probably moved back with her mother, Connie, in Ogden, Utah. Her mother could then help with the two small children so she could take care of her affairs.

Mary Flora Cisneros Holbert(my mother)

Mary Flora Cisneros Holbert, Kelso, California, 1950's

4. MY JOURNEY

My desire to confirm and find evidence of my heritage was instilled in me at a very young age, and not having a close relationship with my stepfather encouraged me to seek the truth. I would snoop around in my mother's old paper work and storage boxes that she kept downstairs. That was where I first found a baby book. It was your typical baby book with name, weight, color of eyes, father's information, first tooth, and so forth. It was my baby book, and it was about ten pages long. The front said, "Baby Book for Perline," and it had "Buck Casper" recorded as the father. I hid it downstairs and went to get JoJo to show her the book. I can't remember which of us suggested it, but we took it upstairs to ask our mother why there was a different father's name in my baby book. My mother quickly took it from us, and the next time we saw it, she had erased "Buck Casper" and had written "Harry Holbert" in as my father's name. This confirmed I indeed had a different father, so my desire to search was intensified.

My debut in this world was made at 12:45 o'clock A.M. on _____ day, the 10 of December, 1955 at _____ My Doctor's name was Dr. P. C. Starke _____

The color of my eyes Blue my hair Black and my complexion White

Mother and Daddy named me Paul _____ because _____

My Baby Book

My mother had an old green suitcase in which she stored pictures, letters, and old paper work, so I decided I might discover something inside it. I did find an official name change, and it was mine. I remembered the name change was something that began with "C," but I really couldn't remember if it was Casper. I was so excited I ran upstairs waving this piece of paper around saying, "Yes, I was right—I do have a different father." My mother snatched it from me, ran into the bathroom, locked the door, ripped it up, and flushed it down the toilet. From that day on, I was positively convinced I had a different father.

My childhood was not a happy childhood, but I was a good student and received good grades in school. It was a better environment in school than at home, so I was rarely sick. I remember one semester I brought home straight As and one B, and my mother yelled at me for the B. I thought this was a good report card, and other classmates would tell stories of how their parents were proud of them for such good grades. The next semester I was determined to act out and show my mother how bad I could be. My best friend, Karin, and I had already made plans to try out for cheerleading. Unfortunately this was the semester I needed good grades to get into the program. I didn't turn in my homework and acted up in class, and, therefore, I produced bad grades. The only thing that this experience showed me was that my mother really didn't care, and the only one it hurt was me because I could not try out for cheerleading because of my grades

My home life had gotten worse. I had a boyfriend named Don Mattson and we were inseparable. I got pregnant at 15 and married Don. We moved in with Don's family. I think a lot of the reason I did this was to get out of a horrible alcoholic and

11

abusive upbringing; this was my escape, my salvation or rescue, or however you want to see it. Don and I struggled but finished high school by going to night school. We worked as dishwashers at a nursing home with my mother-in-law. As my journey continued, I found that living with the Mattson's, a normal, stable family, presented difficulties as I tried to adjust. Mr. and Mrs. Mattson, Don's father and mother, accepted me and welcomed me into their family. I am not sure if they were aware of my childhood or knew how dysfunctional I was or that I was so uneducated about the minor things in life. They showed me how a normal life can be with a normal family, and for this I have always been grateful.

I was working at the Golden Manor Rest Home in the kitchen with my mother-in-law, Belva. Don and I had the afternoon shift, and worked together until he got a job at JC Penny's. Our job consisted of serving dinner, washing dishes, and cleanup. I received a call from my mother saying that my stepfather, Joe, was threatening to tell JoJo that he was not her father. My mother was on one of her binges at the time. I didn't know anything about JoJo having a different father and always thought Joe was her dad. So this was news to me.

It was at the busiest time of my shift and I said out of the blue, "Well, you might as well tell me about my real father, too." To my surprise she told me the whole story; I remember standing there with my mouth wide open, shocked by what I was hearing. She had always denied that I had a different father.

5. THE REVELATION

The story my mother told me was that my father was Buck Casper. He was from Albuquerque, New Mexico, and at the time was married or separated. He was a friend of her first husband, Harry, and helped her when Harry died. He worked for a railroad company in Kelso, California. He had two boys with his wife, and he and my mother agreed that she would have me but felt she would be better off without him. Apparently, he was going through a difficult separation or divorce.

She would have money from Harry's estate and be financially okay, so before I was born, she moved to Utah to be near her mother. My mother had issues with Harry's estate—problems with his social security number or something, so it took several trips back and forth from Utah to California to get all the paper work completed. She said when she went back on one of these visits, Buck had left. Some people said they thought he'd gone to Alaska, but she just figured it was to get away from his wife. She also said that she wrote letters to him off and on. He

13

was aware that she was pregnant with me. My stepfather was a jealous man, and he destroyed the letters and pictures my mother had of both my father and JoJo's father.

6. LIFE CONTINUES

After seven months of marriage, my first son, Don, was born. Three years later I had another son, Brandon. When I walked on stage to receive my high school diploma, I was five months pregnant with Brandon. So at the young age of 19, I had two boys, was working at the rest home, and graduating from high school. My marriage started to take a bad turn as I found myself in a very abusive marriage; I was married to an alcoholic. I divorced Don and, while waiting for the divorce to be final, I met a man named Curtis Colvin who treated me well and appreciated me. After all the abusive outbursts from Don, telling me no one would want me and I was just an ugly Mexican, I fell for Curtis. I guess the books would say it was "rebound love".

Curtis and I were married and my divorce and marriage announcement was printed the same day in the local newspaper. My marriage to Curtis didn't last long. I am sure it had a lot to do with it being a rebound love or the fact that he had two boys from a previous marriage and I had mine. The pressures of this at such a young age wore on us, and we decided to divorce. It was a mellow, agreed-upon divorce, and we even celebrated with our friends in a bar. I dated Curtis off and on and always wondered if we hadn't had all our obstacles if maybe we would have made it.

In my early 20s, I got a job with Ogden City as a secretary and was going to school at night when I decided I wanted to try to find my real father. This was back in 1979 when computers and the Internet weren't available as they are today, but between schoolwork, my daily work, and raising two children on my own, I made my first attempt. I decided to send a letter to the railroad company; the Social Security Administration; the vital records office in San Bernardino, California; Dear Abby; and the Salvation Army. I had to research all the addresses and agencies and type all the letters, and this took some time, but one by one I completed each task. After all these attempts, I was told from all these resources that without a real name (Buck was his nickname) or social security number, they could not help me. I was discouraged and out of ideas.

Time went on, and my federally funded job with Ogden city was coming to an end. I started going to college full-time during the day and lived on unemployment checks and grants for school. I met my third husband, Mitch Hicks. He was a bartender in a bar that I played women's softball for, and we hit it off. I got pregnant, and seven years after the birth of my second son, I gave birth to another son and named him Forrest Hicks. I realized soon into this marriage that it wasn't going to work, but I found myself pregnant again with my only daughter, April, which was a blessing because she was the cutest thing you ever saw.

I applied for a government job and worked various small jobs to try to bring in extra money. I had to drop out of college because I just didn't have the support from Mitch or my family to help me with the kids. After a year I finally got a job with the government at Hill Air Force Base—I was six months pregnant with April, my last child. My first job at Hill Air Force Base was as a keypunch operator, in the supply area-the lowest entry-level job there was, but I continued to work swing shift job which was three to eleven p.m... Working a swing shift job, was difficult for me with a family. My daughter, April, was born in January, and I then had four small children, one being an infant .

I also played softball, and softball season was coming up, and I wasn't going to be able to play if I was working a swing shift. My friend Kathy on my team knew John Kenny, the Director of Material Management (a hot shot), who was also a softball player. She asked him if he knew of any openings for a day shift job so I could still pitch for our team. He also was a pitcher and could appreciate the need to play softball. John found me a secretarial day shift job and told me to just show up without an interview. I guess since I was a pitcher for a softball team, was a good enough interview for him. It was a good thing I had secretarial experience and knew how to type.

John pitched for a coed team on the Base, and later on I was asked to pitch for his team because he was going to be out of town. So I agreed to play in his place. I showed up with my bat and mitt, and his team mates, mostly male, teased me about showing up with my own bat. As if they were questioning my softball playing skills. They were used to John's style of pitching-he never moved from the pitcher's mound. When I pitched I always covered home, first, and third bases. There was a pop-up fly ball between home and the pitcher's mound, and I went to catch it, and the catcher ran after it, too, and we collided. I ran over the catcher, and we both fell, and he ended up with a cut on his forehead. The team came running to pick me up instead of the injured player (that's before chivalry was dead). I told them I was okay, but the catcher was bleeding. I think I impressed my team-mates with my softball abilities. The next day at work in the cafeteria during lunch, I heard them whispering,. "That's her-- the one that ran over the catcher, and he needed stitches. "

This is when I tried again to search for my father. This time I sent out letters to all the Casper's who lived in California and Alaska. The letter read that I was trying to locate a family relative of Buck Casper. The letter included information I had about him. I wrote that he passed away and has left a large inheritance and it was important to locate his next of kin to resolve his estate. I never got any responses from this effort, probably because of the unlikelihood of this happening or the unprofessional attempt of the letter.

S. J. Casper

SI 261B Dakota NE

Albuguerque, New Mexico

To whom it may consern:

    We are interested in locating Buck Casper. Who we believe
to have worked with the Railroad in or around Keslo California.
Approximately 22 years ago. An acquaintance of Mr. Casper has
passed away leaving Mr. Casper in the will. This Estate cannot
be settled until Mr. Casper can be located or next of kin, in
the event of his absense by death. The information we have thus
far has led us to believe Mr. Casper originated in Albuquerque,
New Mexico.

    If you have any information that could lead us to Mr. Casper's
whereabouts could you please contact us so we may resolve this
matter as soon as possible.

                              Sincerly yours,

                              Perline Colvin
                              Perline Colvin
                              609 E. 1225 N.
                              Ogden, Utah 84404 U.S.A.

7. HARRY (BUTCH) PORTER

When I got my day job as a secretary, April was around a year old, and I met Harry (Butch) Porter. He was a supervisor down the hall and was 17 years older than I was. He apparently was going through a bad marriage, and his secretary introduced us in the copy room while she was showing me how to operate the machine. He was bringing her a letter to copy and send out. I'd told her he looked like a silver fox. He was balding on top with almost all-gray hair, a beard, and mustache going gray with shades of black. He had a good build and seemed like a man with a sense of humor because as he leaned over to sign the letter, he had a funny face drawn on the top of his partially bald head. His secretary told him about my "silver fox" statement, and he started visiting me and stopping by my desk, and then we started taking walks during lunch and going out to lunch. I sat in a large open area with many desks, sat next to my boss, Paul. When Butch would come visit, my boss thought he was coming to see him and he would offer him his chair. Little did he know that Butch was visiting me. My coworkers would giggle because they knew he was visiting me, not Paul. He would bring me little mind puzzles to figure out. I don't think I ever figured them out, but he would.

During this time I started searching for my father again. So over the next few years, off and on, I would look up Caspers and call them and ask questions, but I never found any leads. I even made another attempt at sending a letter to many of the Casper's who lived in California and Alaska, but this time I decided to tell the truth. I explained my situation and only got one response back. It said that I should try the Alaskan pipeline—that a lot of men went to Alaska to work on the pipeline or railroad in the mid-50's. So every two to five years I would get a wild hair and look again for him. I accumulated lots of paper work from all these efforts and kept the papers in a file.

To Whom it may Concern: date: 23 July 1996

I am trying to locate or find any information on a Buck Casper, originating in Albuquerque, New Mexico. I understand that Buck is a nick name and not his birth name. The only information I have on Mr. Casper is he worked for the railroad in 1954 in Kelso or Barstow California. He was separated or getting a divorce from his wife at that time. He had two sons from his wife. I estimate his age today to be late 70's or early 80's. My mother said she thought that he had quit the railroad and was going to Alaska.

I have reason to believe that he is my biological father. My mother at the time was Mary Holbert residing in Kelso California. Buck was an acquaintance of my Mothers first husband, Harry Holbert. He passed on and Buck helped my mother with the arrangements etc. I am interested in any information of Mr Casper not only for genetic reasons but personal. I am married and name is Perline Lisa Porter, age 40, born Dec 10, 1955 in Ogden, Utah. I have long straight dark brown hair, hazel eyes, 5 ' 3", weight 135. I was told I resembled Buck. I have 4 children and 1 grandson. I live in Layton, Utah and have a very good job as a computer Specialist for the Mega Center here at Hill AFB, UT. I have always wanted to know and have tried several other avenues to try to locate any information on Mr Casper. I know I have two half brothers and would be very interested in knowing about them and their lives.

The other options I have tried are: Union Pacific Railroad Company, Omaha, NE; County of Bernalillo, Albuquerque, New Mexico; Birth and death records , Washington D.C.; Los Angeles County Clerk; Genealogical Depart, Salt Lake City, UT; Salvation Army, Rancho Palos Verdes, California; R.L. Polk Co, Kanas City, Mo and Dear Abby. As you can see I have tried and tried and found nothing. I think it is because Buck is a nickname and I do not know his real name. Also I do not have a SSN , Drivers License or picture. I think Buck is a nickname for Charles or Anthony but I guess it could be for almost any name.

I would appreciate any Information on Mr Casper or name, address, phone of any of his children etc. or anyone that might know of him, whereabouts or just information on him..

Perline Porter
phone:

Time went by and I divorced Mitch in March 1984, and Butch divorced his wife Frances and Butch and I got married, October of 1985. We struggled with raising my four children and his youngest son. We even picked up an extra - my niece Kari Reed, who was four years old when she came to live with us. We brought her into our home and took over guardianship of her. Her mother, my half-sister Debbie, was in and out of mental institutions, and Kari was being passed back and forth among my mother, my brother Todd, and I; so Butch and I finally decided we would keep her and raise her as our own. We had our struggles and nearly divorced, but we continued on. The difficulties of raising stepchildren are always a struggle, but Butch and I prevailed.

8. SPRING BREAK TRIPS

I had known about the Kelso Depot from my mother. It was where my mother had conceived me, and I wanted to visit the Depot. When my children were young, probably the mid-1990s, we were taking them on short trips during their spring breaks from school, to different National Parks to discover Utah. We had a trailer we would use and I convinced Butch that Kelso, California would be one of our trips. Kelso was in the middle of the Mojave Desert. I remember my children would ask, "Why are we in the middle of nowhere?" I would just say, "It is an adventure—enjoy the ride."

When we arrived at the Depot, it was fenced off, the windows were boarded up, and it was being either demolished or restored. So there wasn't much to look at, but we took pictures and walked around. The boomtown that was there in the past had only a few foundations and bricks left. There was a paper posted about a ghost that haunted the area after being shot. It said the ghost could be seen still roaming the area. It was weird seeing this huge Spanish Mission Revival-style building in the middle of nowhere, with palm trees in front and lush green grass and railroad tracks. We drove a few miles into Cima, California, and stopped at the store/post office there. I asked the lady who ran the post office questions about Harry Holbert. She said she remembered him and that her late husband spoke of him. Then we went to the store side to buy a treat for the kids, and there she was again as she ran both the little store and post office.

Life continued I would try periodically to search for information about my father, but then I started researching the Kelso Depot and its history and found lots of interesting information. I found out that after our first visit to the Depot, there was a big effort Statewide to save the Depot from being demolished, and the Union Pacific Railroad donated the Kelso Depot to the Bureau of Land Management (BLM). Monies were raised to renovate the building and turn it into a historical visitor center. In 2005 renovation was completed, and it was turned into a visitor and historical center. I really wanted to go and see this because my previous trip was so disappointing with it being boarded up; I hadn't been able to walk inside and see it in its glory.

Picture of Kelso on our first visit

9. KELSO DEPOT

Cima, California, is a small boomtown about two miles from Kelso, California, in the middle of the Mojave Desert. Kelso Depot was a helper-station train depot and was a bustling boomtown through the 1920s to 1959. During the war in 1942, the Kaiser Steel Company opened the Vulcan Iron Ore Mine to mine iron to help support the war efforts, and also the train helped transport the metals to the factories. The town population surged to between 1,500 and 2,000. The railroad upgrade from Cima Hill to Kelso was the halfway point from Los Angeles and Salt Lake (L.A. and S.L.), the Union Pacific train route, and a stopping point to fill up with water and to rest. The railroad built a huge Spanish Mission Revival-style depot to support the railroad workers. It had a restaurant, rooms to board railroad workers, and a telegraph office, and it also served as a meeting and dance hall for card games and church services. It was a beautiful Spanish style building sitting in an oasis in the Mojave Desert.

Kelso depot on our second visit

10. MY SECOND ADVENTURE TO KELSO DEPOT

I talked to my friend Belinda Taylor (Bell), and we decided to take a road trip to see this place after it was saved and restored, and there was something to see. I had first asked Butch to go, but he had no desire to go because of our previous adventure. So Bell and I went on our road trip. We decided that we would combine this trip with checking out retirement places, also, since we were getting close to retirement age.

We made our reservations in Mesquite and Las Vegas, Nevada, and Lake Havasu, Arizona. We put our destinations addresses into Bell's GPS and off we went. We drove to Las Vegas, spent the night, drove into Kelso the next day and then to Lake Havasu.

When we got to Kelso Depot, it was beautiful; it had been renovated and was really nice. It was converted into a visitor center, and the two huge Palm trees were still there. The visitor center had all the setups and displays as it had been when it was a booming town. The fence was no longer there, and the

31

windows were not boarded up. It was painted and looked so original. Inside the depot they had a miniature display of what the city looked like back in the 1950s, all kinds of videos of conversations with old-timers talking about the Kelso Depot, the history of the railroad, steam engines, and information about the desert. The Depot had a restaurant called the Beanery, and it was renovated to its original or almost original state. The Beanery previously served many wonderful meals and fed the railroad workers; it was also a stop for many travelers going thorough to their destinations. There were lots of old railroad artifacts, clothing of the time, and even the dishes that were used in the original restaurant. It apparently was one fine restaurant and very famous in its time.

Upstairs there were rooms where the railroad workers slept. The rooms were set up for display to look as they did back in the past. It was very interesting, and we went through the whole place absorbing every last detail. As I was leaving, I asked the receptionist some questions, and she gave me a thick book titled, *An Oasis for Railroaders in the Mojave: The History and Architecture of the Los Angeles and Salt Lake Railroad Depot, Restaurant and Employees' Hotel at Kelso, California, on the Union Pacific System: Kelso Depot Historic Structures Report*. It was about the Kelso Depot renovations and the saving of the Depot. I took the book and read it. In between the drawings, technical papers, and work of the improvements, it had little chapters about the people of Kelso. In this book I found a paragraph about Harry W. Holbert (my mother's husband), the owner of a local store/bar, dying on the Kelso Depot lawn of a heart attack in April 1954. It also mentioned how the bar gave problems to the constable in town. I also found a few paragraphs that said a work crews, paint crews, and electricians were completing the renovating of the Beanery in March/April of 1955, the same time I was conceived. I took special note of that information as it definitely might be a lead to who my father was- maybe one of these workers.

I think this book motivated me even more, and I tried to contact some of the people who wrote the book such as Gordan Chappel and Dennis Casebier. Dennis Casebier established the Goff School House, which is a museum of the Mojave Desert. He also wrote books about the desert. I contacted him to see if he had any information about a Buck Casper or Harry Holbert. It always came down to Buck being a nickname and not his real name. Mr. Dennis Casebier sent me a copy of a little paper document written by a Mrs. McCoy. Her husband was the constable and telegraph operator at Kelso. They had lived pretty much their whole life in Kelso and raised many children. It was about the lives and people of Kelso Depot from 1952 to 1959. In her story she had a page covering about a 50 of the people living in this community. My mother was listed on this page as "Mary Holbert, & 2 children,------------ widow of Harry Holbert, store keeper before the Browns. She was a Mexican girl". Off and on I would go back to this list and research the males. I researched a lot of the names on this list, but Mrs. McCoy did not put their full names in the documents. She listed names like "Main Line Jones"-----------Locomotive engineer, lived in the railroad club house", or a friend of some person, and I am sure it meant something to her, but the descriptions and names of these people were very vague. I was able to find the voting records of the time. The names did match up with those on Mrs. McCoy's list, but there were also some additional names she did not mention on her page. She described the life in Kelso during that time period and detailed some events that were sad and some were humorous.

PERSONS LIVING AT KELSO, CALIFORNIA
From--1953-59

Pat Larson--Woman Telegraph-operator

Mr. & Mrs. Williams
3 boys & 1 girl (grown)--------------------He--Round-house foreman
                                          She-Homemaker

Clem & Clara Hammond-----------------------He--R. R. Engineer
                                          She-Homemaker

Vorval & Children--------------------------Divorced daughter of Clem
Sidney, Barbara & Anna   & Clara Hammond

Jack & Francis Penney & children----------He--Signal maintainer
Mitch & Sharon   She-Homemaker

Joe Leroux---------------------------------Telegraph-operator

Mr. & Mrs Finnell & children--------------He--Section foreman
Larry, Jerry, Caroline & Marilyn   She-Postmaster & Homemaker

Joe Merrow---------------------------------Local Freight Agent

Mary Tyler & children----------------------Provided meeting place for
Luther, Junior & Joe   Mexican Nationals & helped the
                                           manage their money.

Grandmother Tyler--------------------------Mary's mother

Mrs. Smith---------------------------------School teacher at Kelso
                                           until 1954.

Mrs. Jackson-------------------------------School teacher after 1954.

Mr. & Mrs Aaron Francis & children--------He--Locomotive fireman
Arthur & Kathy   She-Homemaker

John & Marty & girls-----------------------He--Worked on railroad
                                           She-A woman who drank too much

Mr. & Mrs. Brown---------------------------Store keeper & wife until 1955

Janie & Bill-------------------------------Store keeper & wife. She was a
                                           X "Madam."

Mike Rapalli-------------------------------Section foreman at Brant.

Mr. & Mrs. Ed Plummer & 4 children--------He-A rancher & she died of
                                           polio in 1954.

Mary Holbert & 2 children------------------Widow of Harry Holbert--Store
                                           keeper before the Browns.
                                           She was a Mexican girl.

Mike Valdez-----------------------------------Section man

Faye & "Tubby" Ambrose---------------------He--District lineman
                                           She-Homemaker

Don Matson----------------------------------One of Mary's friends.

Bill Sorenson-------------------------------Freight Agent after Joe Merrow.

Wayne & Louise Mathews & 3 boys-----------He--Worked for the railroad
                                           on the B & B gang.
                                           She-Homemaker

Bill Pratt----------------------------------Judge, Kelso Judicial District

Ben & Alberta Shirley & children----------He--Machinist helper. Round
Leonard, Ernie, Bobby, Melvin,   house employee.
Linda & Bengie   She-Homemaker. They were
                                           Najavo Indian. Our very dear
                                           friends.

Johnny Payne-------------------------------Locomotive fireman

"Main Line Jones"--------------------------Locomotive engineer. Lived in
                                           railroad club house.

Slim Morrison------------------------------Night chef at beanery. We
                                           believe he was John Waynes
                                           father. (The actor)

Mr. & Mrs. John Kincaid--------------------He--Signal supervisor
                                           She-Homemaker. Died of sugar
                                           diabetes in 1955.

Joe Holland--------------------------------Constable at Yermo, California

Mr. & Mrs. Van Buskirk & family-----------Signal maintainer before Jack
                                           Penney.

O. R. Warner & Naomi-----------------------He--Locomotive machinist. Years
                                           before he was the constable
                                           at Kelso.
                                           She-Homemaker

Mr. & Mrs. Vic Leonard & daughter Vicki--He--Locomotive electrician
                                           She-Homemaker

Mr. Casebier gave me some names to contact and I did. One was a man who lived in Idaho. I talked to him, and he sent me some pictures he had, but he didn't know who the people were in the pictures. He was a small boy at the time and couldn't remember much now. He gave me the name of another man who was writing a book about the Mojave Desert, and he had some information, too, but nothing specific that I was looking for. He was going to have a major heart surgery and I never heard back from him. I also ordered some books online about the railroad and searched for more information on the area. I also contacted a librarian and had her search the railroad information on Casper, but she never found anything. I joined Archives.com to search about the Kelso area. My husband and I went to our local railroad museum in Ogden, Utah, for a day trip. We went through many magazines and files but never found anything.

11. MY BIRTH CERTIFICATE

My birth certificate listed Harry W. Holbert as my dad and his age (42) and place of birth (Kentucky). I noticed that the address on my birth certificate was not the place my mother was living when I was born but was a house my mother bought when I was about five years old. This indicated to me that my name change must have happened after or around the time we moved to a house on Quincy Avenue in Ogden, Utah. I went to the main vital statistics office in Salt Lake City, Utah, to see if I could get my real birth certificate, but they just gave me the same one I already had. I told them that I wanted my original, and they basically said if I was adopted, I would have to hire a lawyer to get the record opened. That didn't make sense because I was pretty sure I wasn't adopted. I tried researching the county and public court records. I also requested a search for any name change from Casper to Holbert. I found nothing, but it was then that my sister and I noticed that my mother looped her o's to look like a's, and all along what I thought was Casper might have been Cosper. I found my birth notice in the paper, and it had Halbert, not Holbert, which also proved my mother's looping o's. JoJo requested my mother's social security records from the Social Security Administration, and again we found that her o's looked like a's. Then I looked at my birth certificate and noticed that Harry was 42, but he died at 52 in April of 1954, and I was born in December of 1955, so he could not have been my father. Also his birth place was recorded as Kentucky, and he was from Missouri, not Kentucky. This proved again that my birth certificate had been altered.

VITAL STATISTICS

BIRTHS

ST. BENEDICT'S HOSPITAL

Gorder — Harold E. and Lesley Hill, Roy, girl, Dec. 9.

DEE HOSPITAL

Housley — Reese and Doris Wild, 1059 9th St., boy, Dec. 9.

Hansen — Denzil W. and Charlene Peck, Hooper, girl, Dec. 9.

Cluff — Gerald L. and Florence Stephens, 583 31st St., girl, Dec. 9.

Rushton — Robert J. Jr., and Joyce Waddups, 343 N. Washington Blvd., girl, Dec. 9.

Judd — Darrel and Leila Lundquist, Randolph, girl, Dec. 9.

Lanchez — Ramon and Lydia Lopez, Anchorage, Clearfield, girl, Dec. 10.

Halbert — Harry and Mary Cisneros, 219 21st St., girl, Dec. 10.

Smith — Dillon and Blanche Drevo, B-12 Victory Rd., Washington Terrace, boy, Dec. 10.

My birthannouncement Halbert not Holbert

I went back to the vital statics office again, and this time I was going to get JoJo's birth certificate, also, for validation of its accuracy. We were both on an adventure to find our biological fathers. The interesting thing was, our mother never gave JoJo a last name. When JoJo was five years old, my mother went back and gave JoJo the last name Cisneros, my mother's maiden name, and she also added Henry Chavez as JoJo's father and changed his birth place from Mexico to Texas. There was an amendment on file of JoJo's change, but mine did not have any amendments. JoJo always suspected that mom never intended to keep her and was contemplating giving her up but changed her mind. Mom gave JoJo my stepfather's name, Garcia, but this was never official, and he never adopted her. So she was told Joe was her father. When JoJo registered for college and needed a copy of her birth certificate. She found out her legal name was Cisneros, not Garcia. This did not surprise her because when JoJo was about 10 years old, she found out Joe wasn't her father when she overheard a conversation between Joe and his brother. She was sleeping in the back seat of the car with Randy and Debbie. Joe's brother asked him which of the three kids were his. Joe thought JoJo was sleeping, and she heard him reply that Randy and Debbie were his biological children but not her.

I explained to the clerk that my mother must have had my birth certificate changed somehow. She looked again and said there was no amendment filed on my birth certificate but admitted that was strange. There is no way Harry W. Holbert could be my biological father when he had died in April of 1954 and I was born in December of 1955. I wrote again to the county to search for any official name change. I always thought this was the time where my mother would be registering me for school and would need a birth certificate to register me. I also believe she put Harry Holbert as the father so she could collect social security payments for me by claiming Harry was my father. Mother was not one to follow rules and always managed to make changes for her benefit. Obviously, no one checked the dates, 20 months difference when Harry died or when I was born, because they would have seen that I must have been an "Immaculate Conception" birth. My older sister, Sheila, would joke about this: "Well, Mom's name was Mary, and her father was born in December, so you could have been an Immaculate Conception birth." So I could still be Harry's daughter and her full sister.

Before my mother died in 1999, I did ask her if she changed my name or birth certificate. She denied that she did. I was hoping she would say yes. Then I could find my official name change on file so I could find Buck's real name. When my mother died, JoJo got some of her pictures. Some of the pictures were of the Kelso time frame, and she had copies made. She brought them to one of our family reunions at our cabin and I remember one was a group picture. The picture had my mother and Harry, her first husband, in the middle and another couple and a bunch of men. It looked like they were in a bar. We would joke about which of these men looked like my father.

Group picture, right to left bottom row Harry and Mom

12. MORE SEARCHING

had joined Ancestry.com over the years, off and on, just to let it expire or just to take advantage of the free month they offered. I'd spent time on the website searching for Buck Casper. Getting information to either call people or send out letters.

Since JoJo didn't know who her father was, she was in the same situation as I was, so we would talk about this off and on, and we always felt a special closeness because of this. I would ask her why she hadn't tried to find her father, and she really didn't have any interest. I think I helped convince her to try, and then she decided that her boys should know their ancestry. So I asked her if she would like to help me find mine, and she said sure.

By this time my husband and I were empty nesters with the exception of a wayward child coming home here and there. My need to find my father intensified.

So in August 2011, my sister and I decided that we

would search again and see what we could find. I had a job that required me to be on a computer all day, so I didn't have the time that my sister did since she was unemployed and could research a lot more intensively. During her research she found some additional resources, or people that said she should join some adopted groups or DNA groups to see if that would help. She found the DNA site called 23andme.com, and we both decided to join it. We ordered our DNA kits and sent them in, but it was going to take five to six weeks to get our results.

In the meantime I researched on Ancestry.com, taking advantage of the free-month subscription and eventually buying a membership. I searched on Ancestry, RootsWeb, Google, People finder, Archives, Spokeo, and various other sources for a Buck Casper or Cosper. I used the age of the father on my birth certificate, 42, as the age of my father, and it placed his birth around 1914. I found several Caspers and Cospers and started folders to keep track. I found a Marvin Gustver Casper, and his nickname was Buck, but the more I researched him and his family, I found he was never in the Kelso area at the time of my conception.

Another one I found was an Oran J. Cosper, and he fit everything my mother had said about my father: he worked for the railroad; was married; was from Albuquerque, New Mexico; had two boys; was a twin; and was nicknamed Buck. I was elated and on a path. I searched even harder and posted on my ancestry boards and other resources. I was contacted from several people on Ancestry.com that knew of Buck (Oran) or were somehow related somewhere up the family tree, and they gave me lots of genealogy about the Cosper lineage. I found his dad's, Paton Cosper's, obituary, and it listed Buck as a survivor. He was married before, and his wife's name was Margret Brown, and his two boys were named Royce and Ronald. I found distant female cousins by posting on Ancestry's boards. Buck was their uncle. They gave me more information, and were very kind and willing to help. They sent me a picture of Buck; his wife, Margret; and his dad and more information about the Cospers' story. I felt like this was my family already. I had so much information and even found a man on Ancestry named Ron Reason and a woman named Debra Salinas, who had histories that went back to Henryck Gasperd/Casber/Cosper, born 2 November 1733, in Dossenheim, Rhein-Neckar-Kreis, Baden Württemberg, Germany. There was an interesting story about Kasper fighting in a duel with a count in Germany over a woman and killing the count and fleeing Germany to England where he boarded the first boat to the United States to avoid prison. There were many stories of the Cospers on wagon trains. They came from a long line of Methodist preachers, and they had many children.

Every day I would update my coworkers on my news and the excitement of my findings, and we would discuss them as we took our daily lunch walks. I would explain every detail on the Cosper family as if I was convinced that this was my family and after all these years, I had found my biological father.

My spirits were high because the Cospers' story was an interesting one, and I might be related to them. I was convinced I was on the right track and craved more and more information on the Cospers' history. I had found Oran J. Cosper's family, siblings, and family trees on Ancestry. There were discrepancies in the family trees, but I learned that some family trees are only

47

as accurate as the person adding the information. I was starting to feel complete. Oran J. (Buck) Cosper had a twin sister named Ora. I researched her and his other siblings and found more and more information. I found out that Buck had divorced his wife, Margret, and moved to Ohio and started his life there. He worked for the railroad in Ohio and married a woman named Gwen. They never had any children, but he helped raise hers. I found a granddaughter or niece who knew him and spoke very highly of him. He never saw his boys when he left and had nothing to do with them after he left. His boys felt abandoned by him and had some very emotional feelings about him. Their mother struggled as a single woman raising two boys on her own. They pretty much dropped their connection from the Cosper side. When Oran was dying, his wife, Gwen, contacted his only living son, Ronald, to see if he wanted to come and see him before he died, but his son chose not to. Oran's other son, Royce, died, and I found the article on how he died. The cousins didn't have the details but said that he was shot in some sort of accident. I found the article in the paper where Royce Cosper was in the Marines in Louisiana, and he went psycho. He took his neighbors hostage and tied them up in their apartment for hours. He finally came to his senses and untied them and let them go and then went inside his apartment and shot himself. I thought this family had gone through a lot of grief and sadness, losing a son in this manner.

After finding the names of the Cospers, the hardest part of my research was trying to find phone numbers and addresses so I could contact them to see if they would take a DNA test to confirm we were related. I would find numbers and call them, and 90 percent of the time, the numbers were disconnected or I had the wrong number. When I did get someone to answer, I would ask my questions, and some were very helpful and others were very cautious of me.

By piecing together information the cousins gave me and researching on the Internet, I was able to find that Buck's son Ronald Lee Cosper was still alive and living in California, not far from where JoJo lives. He was a retired Professor of Sociology. I tried calling him, and he never would answer his phone. I then tried to track down his son, Patrick, and daughter, Michelle, and I found both of them. Patrick's wife answered and suggested I talk to Patrick's sister, Michelle, because she would be more talkative than Patrick. I called Michelle and explained to her why I was calling, that I wanted to know if her father would do a DNA test for me. She said her father had Parkinson's and was like a recluse and lived in a rural area. She said he never answers his phone and kept to himself. Michelle explained that her dad, never knew very much about his dad and he left when he was very young. The only thing he remembered about him was him coming home from work and smelling like the diesel engines on the trains. She didn't want him to do the test and was very protective of him but thought maybe Patrick would take it. I convinced Patrick to do the 23andme DNA test to see if we were related. He finally decided to take the test and paid for it to help me out. Basically 23andme sends a kit, you follow the instructions, spit in a tube, register online, and then mail in the prepackaged tube to 23andme.com. Then 23andme.com notifies you when they receive it, and they give you an approximate time frame for when your results will be complete.

I was so excited, and waiting for the results was killing me. In the meantime I received pictures of Buck (Oran) and

49

looked up his genealogy. I was so excited that I had found my family. Ronald's daughter Michelle (would be my niece) was as excited as I was. I was convinced I'd found my father, and I was craving any information about the Cospers.

The interesting thing was that Buck was an entertainer and played the guitar and sang in the local bars. Michelle had told me that she ran into an aunt of the Cospers, and she had said she remembered Buck coming by her place in Barstow, California and singing around the campfire, and he would frequent the bars, entertaining. Michelle said that when Buck passed away, they sent Buck's homemade guitar to Ronald, his only remaining son. My mother's first husband, Harry, ran a bar, and this could have been the connection. The other interesting thing was that when I was young, in the sixth or seventh grade, my mother was convinced that I had musical talent and wanted me to take guitar lessons. We couldn't find any guitar lessons, so she put me in violin lessons. I really sucked at playing the violin. I think I am tone-deaf. Then she put me in clarinet lessons, and I only had one lesson. I was not musically talented, and I wondered why my mother thought I would be; was it because Buck was musically talented, so therefore I should be musically talented?

13. 23ANDME TEST SITE

O ur 23andme results came in, and we were excited, but there was definitely a learning curve to maneuver through the site. JoJo and I would call each other and discuss things we found, and we were slowly learning how to maneuver. The site showed what my ancestry was, and I was completely surprised. It showed that I was 77.9 percent European, 14.9 percent East Asian and Native American, 1 percent Sub Saharan African, and 6.2 percent unassigned. I was extremely surprised about how much European ancestry my DNA makeup contained. I knew my mother's side was Hispanic, so I was not surprised that the Native American was there. There was so much to learn on 23andme. It had a Relative-Finder option and listed possible relatives that I shared DNA with. You could send them invitations to share genomes/DNA, and I quickly started to do this. I would connect with possible relatives and ask them how to use this site, and I would get all sorts of suggestions. There was one person, besides JoJo, that I had shared a lot of DNA with and really didn't know how important this was at the time. I shared 3.01 percent, sharing seven segments. His name was Samuel Vance

Logan, and his daughter, Stephanie Logan Falls, was managing his account. She was extremely helpful and would give me suggestions on how to use 23andme to figure out how we were related. In the beginning I was convinced my paternal name was Cosper, and I asked her if she had any Cosper relatives in her family tree; she had none. She gave me a link to her family tree and a fan chart of her genealogy. At this point I was fixed on my last name being Cosper or Casper.

Also, 23andme has disease risk, carrier status, and drug response information, which tells if you are at a high risk for diseases like Parkinson's, cancer, or heart issues and what drugs you probably have reactions to or other complications. This information was very interesting to me, and I took these to my primary doctor and had tests run to make sure I was okay. Also, if you are a carrier of diseases, it lists them. I was a carrier for cystic fibrosis, which means I had one of the two markers, and if one of my children got the other marker from their dad's DNA, they would get cystic fibrosis. I found this very interesting, but there are a lot of controversial issues with medical DNA studies, especially if insurance companies use the results to determine whether or not they will cover you for insurance.

Stephanie had been doing genealogy for a long time, and she kept giving me suggestions on how to find out how we were related. In the DNA I shared with her father, there was a large segment of the X chromosome. I was new to DNA research and was trying to figure out a way to use the DNA findings to find my paternal line. A male only gets an X segment through his mother's side of the family, but a female can get an X segment from either her mother or her father. There just cannot be two males in a row, i.e., a father cannot give the X to the son so that is why you can cross out all those entire lineages. I struggled to figure out a way. Basically, I was sending out invitations to share DNA so I could eliminate the ones that showed up JoJo's findings, assuming these would be linked to my maternal side because we shared the same mother. There were many responses from members, and it came down to comparing surnames and finding a surname that linked to theirs and putting them in the area of conception.

I could also download my DNA, put it in a spreadsheet, and sort it by chromosome and many other ways to look for clues on how to best use the DNA data in my search. There were a lot of people who chose to be anonymous, so I could not find their names or send an invitation. Features were being updated on 23andme that included a new Relative-Finder option and a surname sort. I never would find any Caspers or Cospers on my surname sort list, and I found that to be odd because you would think I would find some. Many of the people that registered with 23andme had been doing a lot of genealogy, and they had a large list of surnames. I found this strange and was starting to have my doubts.

I was surprised that I had a lot of African American relatives on 23andme but learned that all of us originated from Africa and were traced to one African woman. There was a show airing on the History Channel about DNA studies and about how DNA proved that we all originated from one African woman, and there were only two tribes in Africa.

The History Channel's speculation was that one of the tribes died off from a plague and only one survived. The show was called "The Human Family Tree" by National Geographic, and it was extremely interesting. I did find a Jackie Williams on 23andme that was "a woman of color" (as she put it). She knew that her great-great-grandmother was a slave, her father was her owner, and his surname was Carr. Apparently, there was a lot of that going on in the time of slavery, and it could be very common to have a African American ancestor somewhere.

I was also experimenting with other sites like Gedmatch.com. I downloaded my DNA and uploaded it to Gedmatch and created my kit number. Gedmatch is a free site and combines DNA results from many DNA sites like 23andme and Family Tree DNA(FTDNA), but it is not as robust as 23andme. I would list by kit numbers, and I found some relatives on this site, but usually they were also a 23andme member. If the kit started with an M, then you knew they also had a 23andme membership. You could download to spreadsheets and look for their e-mail accounts and names and search on 23andme and see if they showed up there. I was able to find a lot of 23andme anonymous members this way and ask them to share genomes with me. I met many interesting people, and they would give me all kinds of suggestions and help me out on my research. Gedmatch had many utilities—triangulate, chromosome browser, and many more—comparing with others and graphical views of your DNA. I also joined the Ancestry DNA and ordered kit. Also I joined Family Tree DNA site by sending my DNA raw file from 23andme. I was finding that each DNA site had its advantages and disadvantages and each took a while to learn.

14. RESULTS ARE IN

P atrick Cosper's 23andme results finally came in, and I could hardly wait to find out the truth—that his dad was my half-brother. To my surprise it showed that I was not related to him, and if he was a nephew, like I thought, he would have had a high percentage of shared DNA. At first I was speculative, thinking 23andme made a mistake and this couldn't be. As your results come on 23andme, it is not odd to have a few days to a week lapse in seeing the full results. I was convinced this was the case, but a week and then another week went by and no Patrick Cosper showed up. I sent him an invite to share DNA, and we shared nothing. I had been so sure I'd found my roots, but it wasn't so. I was extremely disappointed and notified Michelle that we were not related. She, too, was disappointed and even said we could still be friends and that if I was out in her area, she would like to meet me. I also notified Patrick, but I think he already knew, and I even hinted that maybe he wasn't his father's son. He wished me luck and was sorry it didn't turn out like I'd hoped. I even sent 23andme a message, asking if its testing could be incorrect, but DNA does not lie. I had to believe the truth: Patrick was not related to me, and his dad, Ronald Lee Cosper, was not my half-brother, and Oran J. (Buck) Cosper was not my father. DNA does not lie.

15. MY NEW RESEARCH

Several weeks went by, and I was so depressed thinking that I would never find my father, but after more encouragement from JoJo, I decided I wasn't going to give up. I went back to the drawing board on Casper and Cosper surnames and pulled out the other folders I was collecting. I also found a Bush Cooper (Buck). I did lots of research on them, and it wasn't hard to get off on a tangent and follow other links. I started wondering if my father may have been a friend of Harry's. If I found Harry's obituary, maybe there would be something in it, but I never found it. I did find a relative of his on Ancestry.com and did communicate with her. Pat Crawford was Harry's fourth cousin three times removed. I found out that Harry Holbert was married before and had other children before my brother and sister. I wrote to my older sister and told her what I found, but she was not interested in finding any of her relatives. I found that to be interesting. She was aware that I wanted to know everything and know my roots and where my ancestry originated from, but she didn't care about hers. She was quite satisfied to know who her father was, and she knew her father's name.

JoJo was getting involved in adoption boards and thinking we had similar stories as adopted people. She joined a group which were called, "Search Angels", who helped people search for their families' and answer DNA questions. She read many stories about people having success. People would write that it is possible to find relatives by having a high percentage of the X chromosome and tracking it through the maternal line. She kept telling me that Samuel Vance Logan, second cousin and highest relative on 23andme besides her, shared so much of the X chromosome, and he was my link. She had posted general questions about this, and they all said, yes, it is possible. I had a higher than usual shared X with Samuel, and others had found their ancestors with less shared DNA, so I could definitely use it to find my biological father. JoJo decided to post the real stats of the shared percentages of Samuel's and my DNA on a Search Angels post.

I gave up on the surnames Cosper and Casper and the name Buck, and I decided that I needed to track it down by DNA, scientifically. I was very disappointed that what my mother told me, and what I believed to be true, was not true and that I could not count on any of the information. I needed to figure out how to find my roots by DNA and try to understand what JoJo was saying about the X chromosome. I did believe my mother had an affair with Buck, and maybe she truly thought he was my father, but obviously there was someone else.

Stephanie, Samuel Vance Logan's daughter who managed his 23andme account, notified me that she found another relative on 23andme who shared the X chromosome. His name was James Thrash, so we started looking for information on him. He wasn't answering us on 23andme, and his age was up there, so we were thinking that maybe he had passed away. He finally responded to our requests, but his X chromosome was not as large as Stephanie's father's and mine, and basically he did not have the time at that moment to help us. Stephanie also said using his X percentage wouldn't help us much, that her father's was much higher and had better chances.

I started looking at Stephanie's family tree and she sent me a fan chart of her tree. I mentioned to her what my sister had said about the X chromosome, and she sent me her fan chart again with X's and check marks outlining the possibilities. I was corresponding with Stephanie about the exact area I should start looking which meant tracking through the maternal line. It was a little confusing to me at first, and I was trying to make sure I was searching in the right area. This confusion was due to the way the X chromosome gets handed down only through the maternal line.

Fan Chart with X's and check marks

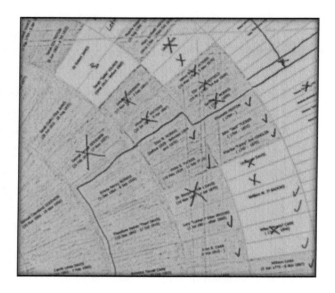

My research started, and I had to follow Samuel Vance. At this time I was just getting ready to retire after thirty years of federal service and was looking forward to spending more time on my journey. Researching history or genealogy is very time consuming and requires a lot of hard work. My husband and I were going to rent a house in Arizona for two months to get out of the harsh Utah winters. This would allow me to spend more time on my research and present me with peace and quiet.

My research started, and I had to follow Samuel Vance Logan's maternal grandmother to find a descendent that was in the area of my conception, and it had to be through her only. It was narrowed down to America Terrell Carr Davis and Emma Nancy Norris Goodwin. I started searching America Carr Davis and all her children, and I was not finding any information on them during the time frame or that they left Louisiana or Arkansas. The Davis and Goodwin families had many children, and tracking down each of them was a very difficult task. This took some time, and I was sending e-mails to various family trees, seeking information. I found a few that had names of value in them. We found a Jacob Lowe, and I wrote to him, but he never replied, and this is how I found Mary Jo. Mary Jo was a member on Ancestry.com, and I found some information on a family tree she posted on the Davis and Goodwin families. I sent her a contact notice, and she responded to me. She sent me some family-tree sheets on the Collins family but wasn't sure how to contact any of them.

Kathy Johnston was another helpful experienced genealogist and she responded to the post on the Search Angels that JoJo posted and found Mozelle Molly Goodwin Collins who married George Edward Collins, and she lived in

Yermo, California. She was the daughter of Emma Nancy Norris Goodwin and the only child who moved from Louisiana and lived in Yermo, California. Emma Nancy Norris Goodwin would have been the next person in my search. The Search Angels were confident this was my family tree and where I was going to find my roots. My father had to be one of Mozelle's sons.

Mozelle had married a George Edward Collins and lived in Yermo/Kelso California. George worked for the railroad and they had four sons: Hugh, Edward, John, and Forest (who passed away at three years old). We started looking at Hugh Lafayette and Edward (Woody) Woodrow and found that they worked on the railroad and were in the Kelso area. Mozelle was the only one through the maternal line who'd moved from the Louisiana or Arkansas areas. We didn't pursue the youngest son, John, because he was born in 1937, and my mother was born in 1930. That would put her six or seven years older than John, and John would have been eighteen years old at the time of conception. We both thought he was too young to be considered as a possible father. We even considered George Edward Collins as a possible father but the X chromosome had to carry through Mozelle, not George, so he could not be a possibility.

Now we had to find some relatives of these men. Mary Jo had information on the Collins family because she was related to them. With her help and more searching, we found Hugh, Mozelle's oldest son. He had one son still living, and his name was Jessie (Rip) Collins. Mozelle's second son, Edward (Woody) Woodrow Collins, had a daughter (Lee Ann Collins Lowe) and a son (Mark) still living. So we searched and searched to find phone numbers or any pertinent information about them. Mary Jo was a cousin of the Collins family from her mothers' side, and she was very helpful and gave me a lot of information on the Collins family's genealogy, but she wasn't sure how to find them. I also found out from the tree that Jacob Lowe had on Ancestry that he was Lee Ann's son. Lee Ann was Woodrow (Woody's) daughter, and he no longer had a membership on Ancestry.com, and that was why he didn't reply. I did find Lee Ann (Collins) Lowe living in Texas, and Rip was living in the San Diego area. The only phone number for Rip was at a company called The Tarp House. I finally called there and asked to talk to Rip, and he answered. I tried to explain to him why I was calling, I was very nervous and excited and my explanation of why I was calling wasn't coming out correctly. I asked if he had an e-mail address that I could write the explanation and send it to him. He said he was at work and real busy, and I could e-mail him or fax it to his work number, and he gave me the number and his home number, too. I typed up a page of explanation and faxed it to the number he gave me and e-mailed it to him.

Letter I faxed and emailed to Rip:

Jesse,
My name is Perline Porter, I live in Layton, Utah and am 57 years old, and married. I am writing to you because I have been searching for my biological father for years. Last year I joined a DNA site called www.23andme.com in hopes of tracking down my father's relatives and find more information on who they are and where they came from. This sight matchs DNA from all over the world that joins and it was very easy and iinteresting. You meet all kinds of people that you share DNA with. I found a Samuel Vance Logan which shared a large amount of the X chromosome and others. With lots of help and searching we have found your family and think that one of the brothers Hugh or Woody was my father. We traced the lineage back thru Sam's

grandmother and thru the female line (X chromosome only follows the female line) and location of where I was conceived which was Yermo/Kelso area in California in the Feb-March, 1955. My sister JoJo, also found a group of genealogist, called the "search angels" and they lead us to your family. All the other linages, for example, America Terrel Carr and her family, born, lived in Louisiana and never left Louisiana and I had to find a female that did and it is your grandmother Mozelle. I was just getting ready to search Emma Norris's children and grandchildren when I ran into a Mary Jo's family tree, which is related to you on the Belvins side. She has done lots of research and shared some of the Collins information with me. She has been also helping me find you.

I know that you were a very young boy at this time, 8 years old and probably don't remember much but anything would be helpful.
If you have any pictures of Hugh or Woody or anything I would truly appreciate it or share memories etc. that you can remember.

I would really like to explore this a little more and in order to do that I need a male, to join 23andme and see if you are indeed my uncle. If you would PLEASE go to the site and check it out. They just lowered the price from $299 to $99 and that is a great deal. If you do not have the funds to do this I would be willing to buy a kit for you. They require a monthly fee of $9 for a year and I would pay that too if you are interested and do not have the funds. I have really enjoyed this site and met many interesting people and found out lots of information about my ancestry and your family. It also gives your health and disease risks information too, if you are interested, you can opt not to get that info but I found it to be very beneficial.

My mother, Mary Cisneros Holbert, was married to Harry William Holbert and he ran a store and bar in Cima, which is about 2 miles from Kelso Depot, a train depot in the Mojave desert. Harry died in March of 1954 of a heart attack on the Kelso lawn. My mother told me that my father was a friend of Harry's and was married or getting a divorce and had two boys. He helped her in her time of grief and is my biological father. She told me his name was Buck, but Buck is a nick name and I have been looking for years with hardly any info and

64

my sis JOJO turned me on to this DNA site.

I tried to find your phone number but only found an old one that is disconnected and hoping that this email is correct. Please feel free to call me and we can talk more about this and I can send you any information that I have gathered so far. My home phone is 801-XXX-XXXX and my cell is 801-XXX-XXXX or give me your current phone number and will call you.

I really would like to get to know you and would GREATLY appreciate your help.

This is the line that I followed to fine you and so thrilled and hoping you will help.

Emma Norris > Mozelle Goodwin > Edward Woodrow Collins >

Me
or
Emma Norris > Mozelle Goodwin > Hugh Lafayette Collins >Me
or
Emma Norris > Mozelle Goodwin > John Mason Collins Sr. > Me Don't think John is a possibility too young in 1955.

He called me later and said that he read my fax and found it interesting, and he knew Lee Ann's number and would call her to see if she would like to talk to me. He said he would forward my e-mail to her. Rip sounded like a character. I did talk to Lee Ann about my journey and she was very cooperative and helpful. Later Rip said that I had gotten Lee Ann excited about my search. They gave me Lee Ann's brother Mark's number, saying he knew a lot about the family and was quite the talker. He was in a nursing home in Barstow, California, and I tried calling to talk to him, but he didn't sound too well and was having a difficult time hearing me. Mark finally told me he wasn't feeling well and to call another time. Rip told me Mark was just recovering from mouth surgery from cancer. Lee Ann said that he would probably do the test, but I suggested I would rather have her, she just sounded more dependable.

I called them and explained my situation to them and asked if they would be willing to do a DNA test with 23andme and told them I would pay for the test. They both said yes. Lee Ann's mother died when she was very young. Lee Ann her brother Mark, were raised by their uncle Hugh and Mary was raised by John Sr. and his wife Susan. I was again excited that I was on another lead. Rip sent me an e-mail asking what they wanted for this test— hair, blood, or sperm?

It was the waiting period that killed me, as I am an impatient person. Lee Ann didn't hesitate, but Rip was hesitant. I'm not sure if he was not very computer literate or just lazy, but I kept calling and asking. He would say, "Well, I haven't done it yet." Lee Ann told me he was a sick man, and maybe he was in the hospital; he had extensive COPD. I was e-mailing him, but he was not responding, and I finally started calling him over and over. He finally answered, and during our conversation I basically told him he can't ignore me because we could be family, cousins or siblings, and when he doesn't respond, I get worried. He did tell me he turned in his kit, but Lee Ann and I wondered if he really did because there were instructions that said you had to register your kit online on 23andme before you sent it in. We wondered if he followed the instructions. While I was waiting and getting anxious, thinking it would be soon that I would know whether it was Rip or Lee Ann who was my sibling or cousin, Lee Ann sent me an e-mail saying that Rip had passed away on January 31, 2013, in his sleep. I was devastated. I had just talked to him and e-mailed him and was looking forward to meeting him and Lee Ann.

I contacted his wife to express my condolences and asked if she knew whether Rip turned in his kit or not. She was grieving, but she did tell me that she would look around when she went through his stuff. The good thing is he did not suffer; he went to sleep and never woke up. He was only sixty-five years old. His wife told me his services would be in three or four weeks. Lee Ann told me that the family inherited asthma from their mother's side, and they all basically died from COPD. Her mother and the family were smokers, which did not help.

I tried to get 23andme to tell me whether Rip at least turned his kit in or not, and they basically said they couldn't release that private information. If the family had filled out a nearest of kin paper work request, they would release the information to them. If the family would have just responded with Rip's e-mail account to 23andme and shared it with me, I would have known. I tried one more time to call his wife, but you could tell she was not in her right mind, and my problem wasn't her priority. Considering the circumstances I could understand. I had asked if I could get information for Rip's son, Michael, so I could contact him, and she said she would let him know and see if he would. I asked her to please call me on the services, and she said she would. I found the listing for Rip's funeral services on the Internet. They would be March 6, 2013, and I debated going to them. Rip had one son still living, Michael, and he lived in Arizona with his mother.

I was back in a slump again, but I still had Lee Ann's results, and she sent me an e-mail saying they were in, but she was not showing up on my relative finder. I was starting to get more depressed and thinking I was in for another disappointment. I had sent her a share invitation, which she accepted, and she appeared on my relative finder as a first cousin. She shared 15.5 percent of her DNA with me, which makes her higher than a first cousin but not high enough to be a half-sister. So my journey continued. We were sure Hugh was my father, not Woody. I was really disappointed because of not getting Rip's results from 23andme to determine if for sure he was my half-brother. I was thinking I had a half-brother, and just before I could find out for sure if he was, he died. I so wanted to meet him and get pictures and stories of his childhood and just get to know him. I had been looking for so long only to get this far and have my half-brother die at the age of sixty-five.

I was in a slump again, and I was trying to figure how I could find out if Hugh was my father for sure. I was still not even considering John Sr. For some reason I thought John Sr. was the same as Rip's son, Michael, and would be a nephew, and testing him would not narrow it down enough to determine for sure. If I tested Rip's son, Michael, and John Sr.'s son, John Jr., the percentage of DNA on a nephew or first cousin would be close but would not really tell me anything. My thought was that John Sr.'s son was a nephew. So I was thinking I would have to be satisfied with what I had.

After the DNA test came and confirmed that Lee Ann was my first cousin and I was related to her, I finally confirmed that the Collins were my relatives. I called Lee Ann and asked her if she would like to meet me. We have friends that live in her area of Texas, and we were planning a trip out there in a month or two. She said no and explained that it had nothing to do with me, but she had a similar experience by meeting her half-brother, and it wasn't a good experience and brought some old emotional feelings. Her mother had two children from a previous marriage and apparently she just met one of them. She said she was still not strong and didn't need to put herself through all that again. I was very disappointed and looking forward to meeting her. I'd finally found my roots, and she didn't want to see me. So I was really in the dumps again. Lee Ann said she was a private person, hadn't been very involved with the family, and had pretty much lost contact with them when the grandparents died. She didn't have a good childhood, didn't want to think about it, and only wanted to concentrate on her current family. She said she was a retired schoolteacher, had just finished chemotherapy treatments for colon cancer, and was still weak and had no strength.

I e-mailed Mary Jo and Stephanie about my new discoveries. Mary Jo mentioned again that John Jr. should be tested, and I couldn't see the importance of it, thinking he was a nephew. Mary Jo would say John, Sr. was the youngest, wildest son and a horn dog, and if you knew Hugh, there wasn't a place that Hugh went where his wife wasn't with him—they were inseparable. She had said John Sr. was a horn dog before in e-mails, but I never realized the importance.

I kept telling JoJo that we should look at the John Jr. thing but was not sure if testing John Jr. would give us anything because the difference between a nephew or first cousin would be too close to call. I wanted her to ask her genealogy contacts if a nephew would be higher than a first cousin. I was very confused on the relationship. Then JoJo called and said, "Perl, I think we are missing something here." So we sat and talked, and I drew it out, and sure enough John Jr. would be a good choice to determine if for sure Hugh Collins was my father. John Jr. would be just like Rip, he is a grandson of Mozelle, not a nephew. JoJo and I had ruled out John Sr. as the possible father because of his age. I was confused with the relationship of John Jr and then realized John Jr. is alive and that his DNA results would determine whether Hugh was my father or not, even without Rip's results. If the test results showed he was a first cousin, then Hugh was my dad. If the results showed he was a half-brother, then John Sr. was my father. We had already ruled out Woody as a possible father by Lee Ann's test results showing she was my first cousin. By testing John Collins Jr., it would rule out Hugh for sure. I wasn't thinking John Jr. could be a possible half-brother...too many Johns I guess in that family. JoJo basically slapped some sense into me over the phone and said, "Don't give up now". Get busy finding John Mason Collins Jr.

JoJo and I still had our doubts. How could our mother get pregnant from a man six or seven years younger, and he was only eighteen years old. I thought contacting John Mason Jr. would be a good idea to basically confirm that Hugh was my father, but Mary Jo kept saying, "I think it was John Sr. He was a horn dog." I was reluctant at first but finally got on board, trying to locate John Jr. Lee Ann said she didn't know exactly where he lived, but it was somewhere in the San Diego area.

I was on the research track again with lots of encouragement from JoJo. I tried looking him up on Ancestry.com and found some possible addresses and then compared them on Spokeo.com and found some matches. I called many numbers on Spokeo.com and left many messages on the numbers that were valid. I left messages on e-mails that were valid, but usually the phone numbers they have on Spokeo.com are disconnected, and the e-mails are not valid. There were a lot of listings for "John M. Collins" and "John Collins" in the San Diego area. I found many addresses in San Diego and called them, but many were invalid, so I continued calling and looking through the "John Collins" and "John M. Collins" lists. Sometimes Spokeo.com would have the person's estimated age on its site, and John would be fifty-two years old.

I was just about to give up when I discovered in La Mesa, California, the same address that I found on Ancestry.com, and the number was different. I called it, and someone answered. I asked if this was John Mason Collins Jr., and he said, "Yes, it is, and who are you?" I tried to explain to him the situation, but the more I explained, the more he thought it was a prank or something. I mentioned Lee Ann and Rip, and he knew both of them. I told him to call and ask them about me, but I said he couldn't talk to Rip because he passed away on January 31, 2013. You could tell by his voice he was very skeptical about the whole thing. He said he would call me back after he checked this wild story out.

I sent Lee Ann an e-mail and made a phone call saying, "I found him, and he is going to call you and ask about me." I waited and waited. Two days went by, and I was impatient; I told you I am an impatient person. Then I got a phone call from John, and he said he checked me out and found I was legitimate, and he would do my DNA test. I was so excited and talked to him for a while, and he basically said that if he was a betting man that he would bet it was his dad because he was a horn dog. He said he called his mother, and she had said the same thing. He had talked to Lee Ann about me and researched it out himself through a friend who was a private detective. I got his information to order his kit, and then it was another wait and wait and...I told you I am not the patient one. I also called John Jr.'s sister, Carey, and she was excited, too, and offered to test, but I said I had already ordered one for John. We did talk a lot, and she said, too, it was probably her dad. I was so excited again.

John got his kit in record time and sent it out quickly. I just needed to wait five to six weeks again for the results. John's stepdaughter, Brandi, contacted me on Facebook, and we exchanged pictures and history. I talked to John several times, and he seemed anxious to find out that he may have a half-sister. He only has one sister, Carey, and he has no kids of his own. Brandi is his wife's child, but he always treats her as his own, and she thinks of him as her father. He works for Cox Communications in San Diego and has light-brown hair and blue eyes and is about six foot one. His daughter sent me pictures of him, and I was so excited. Now we had to wait for his results. We expressed that we would like to meet someday.

In the back of my mind, I had always thought of going to Rip's services in San Diego but not knowing anyone and not knowing for sure if he was my half-brother or not, I was hesitant

72

of going. I felt that it would look weird for a stranger to go to a graveside service of a man she never knew. I had asked Harry if he would like to go with me, and he said no. So I knew if I went I would be on my own. Finally, a week away from his services, I decided I was going. I knew if I didn't go, I would regret it all of my life—regret missing an opportunity to meet family from my biological father's side, not knowing for sure if Rip was a half-brother or first cousin. So I made my airline, rental car, and hotel reservations and asked Butch again, and he decided if I really was going that he would go with me. I e-mailed John and told him I was going to Rip's services. I asked him how far from the services he lived and if I could meet him while I was out there.

His response couldn't have been any better. His daughter, Brandi, put pictures of John and other family members on my Facebook page. After I had made my reservation, she sent me a Facebook message saying that John wanted to pick me up at the airport and that I could stay in their guest bedroom and that he wanted to take me to his bowling league and show me off to his friends. I was so happy because I wasn't sure attending the services was a good idea. I was worried if meeting a possible relative before getting the results was a good idea, but then I realized he was related to me—whether he was a half-brother or first cousin, we were related. Lee Ann's DNA results proved that.

16. MY VISIT WITH THE COLLINS FAMILY

The day came for my flight to San Diego to attend funeral services for my possible half-brother or first cousin, Rip, and to meet my other possible half-brother or first cousin, John, and his family. I was so excited and nervous to meet these people. I did not know how it would work out. The Facebook entries from John and Eva's daughter, Brandi, were overwhelming and very sweet and welcoming.

A lot of references regarding meeting families before the DNA results are finalized are not recommended, and people should always wait to meet after the results are finalized. My circumstances warranted the meeting before because I was going to the graveside services of Rip, and John lived in the area, so it sounded like the right time. I felt if I missed the opportunity to meet Rip's son or family, I would greatly regret it.

We stopped at the post office in Beaver Dam, Arizona, to pick up my mail on our way out. JoJo had sent me a book called *"Finding Family"*, by Richard Hill, a very interesting book about an adopted man finding the truth and his biological family. My story and his were very similar but quite different in the paths we took. I started reading this book when I was waiting for my flight. It was a great distraction because I think I would have been an excited, nervous mess.

When we arrived at the airport, John and his wife, Eva, were there to greet us. We hugged and exchanged our excited greetings and proceeded to get our luggage from baggage claim. John had the evening planned, and it sounded like a good one. We were to go to one of their favorite places to eat and then to John's Tuesday bowling night with his friends. The dinner was nice. He had invited some of his friends, and it was very nice too meet them. His daughter, Brandi; her husband, Chad; and their little girl, Starr, were there. We met Harry (which is the same name as my husband) and Matt, and other friends who were there. It was a little uncomfortable, and then, all of a sudden, I jumped up and stepped over Eva in the booth to sit next to John. This surprised everyone and pictures were taken of us together. I gave him a great big hug and a great big Perl smile and pictures were taken. I think that eased everything.

We then were off to the bowling alley. It was the typical bowling alley atmosphere. We ordered some pitchers of beer, and Eva and I started to chat and got to know each other. She was a very friendly person, and I asked her what her ancestry was. It turned out she, too, was Hispanic and part Indian. You could definitely see it in her features. She had a very interesting background, and we had lots of fun. I got to meet lots of his friends and take many pictures. Little six year old Starr was there, and she sat on my lap and proceeded to file my nails for me with my emery board. She was instantly in love with me. I didn't get to talk much with John because he was occupied in his tournament, but he would come over to join in on conversations or take pictures. After that he drove Butch and me to our hotel, and it was around ten thirty. After all the excitement of the day and beers, we were exhausted and went to bed.

Me and my half-brother, John Mason Collins, Jr

March 5, 2013

The services were at one o'clock the next day, and I could tell by some of the comments John had made that he was a little nervous about going. Even though he was Rip's cousin, he had not seen these people for a long time. We agreed that between the both of us, we could handle it, and I was grateful that he decided to come with me.

Butch and I had breakfast, and I continued reading the book JoJo gave me. It was so interesting, that I was breezing through it. John picked us up around noon, and we were on our way to the services. We got there very early, so we just sat in the car and talked as we waited to see who was going to arrive. The first was two Harley motorcycle riders, and one looked around Rip's age. We stepped out of the car and asked them who they were. They said they were friends of Rip's and to not worry because the rest of the family was not Harley riders. Slowly people started to arrive, and John and I would approach them and introduce ourselves. John would always say, "Hi, I am John, a cousin of Rip's, and this is Perl." Then he would go into the short version of our acquaintances, how I just called him a few weeks ago stating that I might be related to him or Rip—half siblings or cousins—and that we were waiting for the results. He would always say, "We are pretty sure it was my dad and not Rip's, but she came out to the services and to meet Rip's family and mine." John and I discussed that most of the people at the services were Louise's (Rip's wife) children and grandchildren and not many members of the Collins family were there—just us and Rip's son.

Finally Rip's wife, Louise, showed up, and we waited until she had talked to a few others, and then John and I approached her. She was very nice, but you could tell when she found out who I was, she had this interesting look on her face. She mentioned she was still looking for evidence that Rip sent in his DNA and pretty much cut us off. Because of the circumstances, she was not there to discuss my DNA journey but the matters at hand. Louise looked totally different than I had imagined, and she seemed quite nice. I found out that she was the one who owned the Tarp House, and Rip had helped her raise many of her children.

We were all waiting for Rip's son, Michael, who was driving from Arizona to attend his dad's services. He apparently had gotten lost and didn't arrive until around one thirty or two o'clock. When he finally arrived, we all waited patiently for him to get to the graveside. He was a tall, thin man in a suit, and his head was shaved. His suit looked like it was large for him, and he had a yellow rose in his lapel. He had a woman with him, and I wasn't sure if she was a girlfriend or just an acquaintance.

The services started, and the preacher was a son-in-law of Louise, and he seemed very personable. He did a very nice service for Rip. It was one of the most welcoming services I had been to in a while. He opened the service and asked if anyone had any memories of Rip, and several work friends spoke up. Apparently, Rip had been sick for a long time, and the doctors only gave him six months to live, but he lasted eight years longer. He never complained of being sick and always joked around with everyone.

Rip liked his fireworks, and many stories were told about how he almost burned down a trailer court with a misfired rocket that skimmed across a lake and landed in the middle of the trailer court across the lake. He quickly told his son "we are out of here" and started throwing things in the back of his car. Michael spoke up and said, "Yeah, I think that we left a lot of our stuff there because Dad was in a hurry." Another story that Michael told was about when Rip was lighting rockets in his front yard and caught the yard on fire. He turned to Michael and said, "I told you to mow the lawn." Another was when he was lighting rockets and had a box of them nearby. His misfired rocket hit the box and exploded all the remaining ones in the box. Some curious watchers were almost hit by the exploding rockets—ducking and dropping to avoid the explosions.

The one thing he requested was that one statement be on the handouts and his headstone. It was, 'R.I.P', RIP, Jesse George Collins. I didn't get the R.I.P until John said, "You know, R-I-P, "Rest in Peace" and RIP his nickname." His wife mentioned to everyone that Rip was adamant it be mentioned at his services. Louise's daughter and son-in-law were having a little potluck dinner at their house, and John and I agreed to show up. We also approached Michael and introduced ourselves. I told him about my story, about Rip's DNA results, and he agreed to help me out. We agreed when we got to the house to exchange e-mails and phone numbers, and he said he would do anything to help me out. He mentioned that he had not seen his dad for a long time and was just planning on a trip out to visit him when his ex-wife needed to be moved at the last minute, and he could not afford to do both. He also mentioned that he lost track of his dad and found him by searching for him on Google where he found the Tarp House. I announced that was how I found Rip, too.

John had made plans for a barbecue at his house after the services, but we had a little time to stop by the potluck as it was close to where John lived. We arrived and were one of the first people to show up. They had a nice spread of food, and I made me a small plate because John was preparing a nice barbecue later. Finally, Michael arrived, and we exchanged information and talked a little about him and his dad. He seemed very nice and willing to help as much as he could. As we were leaving, Louise finally arrived, but we needed to get going.

We finally made it to John and Eva's house, and it was a very nice house. They had converted one room into a bar and had it all decorated similar to a sports bar. He also told us that the bar was built by him and his friend. It was very nice, and you would have never guessed they had constructed it. John and Eva helped run a celebrity golf tournament and had several pictures of him and Eva displayed on the walls of the sports bar. He had to tell us a story about every one of them. He had known many celebrities, and I was impressed. He was an avid golfer, and he had many awards and displays of signed golf balls from many of these tournaments. His front room was set up with a large-screen TV, surround-sound stereo system, and karaoke. His backyard was very nice. It had orange trees full of oranges. There were tangerine, lemon, lime, and banana trees and many more exotic bushes. He had a swimming pool and hot tub; it was definitely a party house. These people seemed to know how to really enjoy themselves.

Carey's son, Travis, was there also and eager to meet me, and he was very nice. He worked for an animal rescue company and was very accepting of myself and Butch. Eva was making guacamole, and John proceeded to barbecue the Carne

Asada meat for our meal. We sat and had a beer and talked, and John and Eva asked Travis, "Doesn't she have the same mannerisms as John's dad and resemble your mom when she was younger?" Soon Brandi and her family arrived with the salsa, and dinner was ready. It was wonderful. Besides the Carne Asada, Eva made homemade Spanish rice and refried beans, an excellent addition to the meal.

John pulled out his Russian fur hat made out of squirrel fur, and I put it on my head. I told them some stories about our Russian friend Vlad, who had stayed with us for a while. I was interpreting the story and impersonating Vlad's high, deep voice, slamming my hand on the table as Vlad would do. Travis looked at Eva and said, "Oh my god, she is related. That sounded just like something his grandfather would do." Little Starr had made a homemade card, and she presented it to me. She was this cute, petite six-year-old girl. Her card expressed her love for me and asked if I wanted to spend the night with her. She had drawn hearts and put stickers and made stick people pictures of herself and me. I immediately noted she drew a very skinny Perl (as stick people drawings usually are), and I thanked her. I made sure to let John and his family know that they were welcome to come to Utah and spend some time with us at our home or cabin in the High Uinta's.

John and Me, March 6, 2013

It was getting closer to the time for us to leave to catch our flight, and Eva reminded John that he had promised to sing karaoke for us. He was reluctant but then went ahead and set up the TV and machine. He sang "Tequilas Sunrise," and he was very good. He tried to put me in his massage chair so I could not move and try to get a video of him on my iPhone, but I caught on to his prank and got out of the chair, with difficulty, and took the video of him anyway. It was time to say our good-byes to Travis and Brandi's family, and plenty of pictures were taken.

Left to right, Butch, Travis, Eva, Brandi, Me, John, Starr and Chad, March 6, 2013

We drove to the airport and hugged John and Eva and thanked them for all their hospitality and told them we enjoyed every minute of their company. We then said our good-byes. When we were on our way home, John sent me a text that said, "Sis, text me when you get home so we can make sure you made it safely, and no matter what the outcome is, we have grown to love you and Butch, and we will keep in touch." How sweet is that?

I kept in touch with him and Carey, and Carey sent me pictures of their father—some were when he was younger and some were when he was older.

I also received a phone call from Lee Ann's brother, Mark, who was in a rest home in Barstow, California. I tried earlier to call and talk to him but never was able to get through, but I received a call from an intern at the rest home telling me to call him because he wanted to talk to me. So I did and we talked for about an hour and half. He was a talker. He told me a lot of information about the Collins family. His stories of his father and uncle Hugh and uncle John were very interesting. When I asked Lee Ann about some of the details, she said that Mark liked to exaggerate the truth a little. I was glad I got the opportunity to talk to him because his health wasn't that good, and he was having issues.

17. JOHN'S RESULTS

The waiting for the results to come in from 23andme seemed to take forever. Usually it only takes five to six weeks, but this time it took eight weeks and waiting was killing me. I would send 23andme e-mails asking when the results would be in and would also have John send e-mail's to them. In the meantime I received pictures of John's father, John Mason Collins, Sr. I was totally amazed by how much he resembled my two boys, Forrest and Brandon. The younger pictures looked like Brandon, and the older pictures looked like Forrest. There was one picture where he had a cigarette in his mouth goofing around, and it seemed like something that Forrest would do. Other similarities were John Sr. had a brother named Forest who died when he was three years old, and my youngest son's name is Forrest. Also, he had a cousin named Pearl, and I'm Perline (Perl). The Collins family also had Type 1 diabetes in the family, and my son Forrest has Type 1 diabetes. John Jr. told me he had heart surgery to fix a hole in his heart, and I remember my son Brandon telling me that his oldest daughter was born with a hole in her heart.

I got a call from John that the results were in, and I was

so excited to see if he was my half-brother or first cousin. Sure enough he was my half-brother and shared 24.9 percent DNA with me, which put him as a half-brother or grandson—23andme gives you estimates on the relationship based on a scale they use. Lee Ann's DNA was a little higher than a first cousin, which the genealogist said this could be on some intermarriage going on somewhere in the Collins lineage. John showed up higher than my half-sister JoJo, and this was such wonderful news. Even though John and his family knew that it was so, this proved it was. They kept saying that my mannerisms and the things I would say sounded just like something John Mason Collins, Sr. would say. It is truly amazing how you can inherit traits from your father without even knowing who he is. I finally know where I came from and found my biological father and family.

18. JOHN MASON COLLINS, SR

I searched and asked questions about my father and found lots of information. He lived in the Kelso/Yermo area with his father, George Edward Collins, and his mother died when he was only fourteen years old. His father remarried, later, a woman named Maria, and she had a boy named Buddy. John's father, George, my grandfather, liked his booze, and so did John. He frequented the bar in Kelso, and that is probably where he met my mother. He never graduated from high school but later received his GED at Grossmont High in San Diego. At twenty-one he married his first wife, Susan, when she was sixteen, and they had two children: John Jr. born February 6, 1961, and Carey born April 16, 1960. John worked as a riveter for an aircraft company called Rohr and later as a truck driver for Global Van Lines and Cal Neon. He liked to frequent the bars and was very abusive to Susan, which resulted in a divorce in 1971. He later married another woman named Karen, but it did not last long. He then met and married Ruthann in 1983, and they were married for seventeen years before his death in 2004. In 2002 he retired, and they moved to Barstow. Before his retirement he drove a dump truck for a company called Bock Construction. He and Ruthann were married in

John's favorite bar, "The Mellow Inn" in El Cajon California.

He was a fun guy and had many friends: Billy Valentine, Bobby Brodssard, and Jim and Judy Crowl. After his divorce from Susan, he continued to see his children every other weekend and was a good father and loved his children. He had a pickup truck with a camper and loved to travel in it. He was a hard worker, and the one thing Ruthann said, was " that he had the prettiest blue eyes you've ever seen". John died in Barstow four days before Thanksgiving on a Monday in 2004. He woke up early as usual and made his coffee. He was reading his paper when he came back to bed, shaking from head to toe, saying he was freezing. He stopped breathing and died from COPD and congestive heart failure. He had been on oxygen full time and had many health issues.

I always thought if I found my father, he would be dead, but I had based that on his birth date being in 1914, but how very close I was to finding him and possibly meeting him. I only missed him by nine years. If I had started down the DNA search earlier, I might have met him. I think about what I was doing in November 2004, and I remember that my daughter's first son, Jaiden, was born on November 16, 2004. As I have only one daughter, I was going to be able to see my first birth of a grandchild. Jaiden was born early and was born with medical issues: he didn't have the corpus callosum portion of his brain and had water on his brain and a cyst. A few weeks after his birth, he was admitted to the Primary Children's Medical Center in Salt Lake City, Utah, for brain surgery. They placed a shunt to release the fluid on his brain. The surgery was a success. The doctors said that a lot of people are born without their corpus callosum and don't even know it and they do just fine. So at the same time my biological father was dying, I was watching a new life come into this world.

John Mason Collins, Sr with beard

John Mason Collins, Sr.

19. The COLLINS LINEAGE

My curiosity of the Collins' lineage inspired me to search and work on my family tree on Ancestry.com. I found that the Collins family came from Ireland, and many of the Collins boys fought in the Revolutionary War and the Civil War. The Collins family spread across Arkansas, Tennessee, Georgia, Louisiana, Virginia, Maryland, and Georgia. I was able to trace Mozelle's lineage, which were the Goodwin and Norris surnames. The Norris family came from England to the Americas. Thomas Norris Sr., was born about 1608 in Congham, County Norfolk, England. He ran away from home as a boy of 11 and went to sea. In those days he probably started out as a cabin boy. As he grew older, Thomas became a sailor and followed the sea for many years. He landed in Nansemond County, Virginia Colony, about 1630 or 1631 and chose to remain in America. He descended from an old family of County Norfolk, England and was the first member of the family to settle in the American colonies. He immigrated to Saint Mary's County, Maryland Colony, about 1634. He was associated with the trading adventurer William Claiborne in 1637.

The Collins, Goodwin and Norris families all had many children and always seemed to name them the same names—John, Thomas, George, Edward. Even the women were named after former relatives. It is very hard to track down their lineage due to this.

I found a story about Temperance Vinson who married James Collins, the Revolutionary War soldier. There was some question of Patrick Collins being her son, but he was a son of a previous wife of James Collins. The story mentions her other children, but Patrick was never stated as being her son or mentioned.

Temperance's father was in question and was David Vinson, but there were two David's back then in Sandy Creek, Franklin, North Carolina, and it was questionable as to which was her father due to all the same names. The two David's were not father and son but uncle and nephew.

The Collinses were Scotch-Irish descent, and John, Sr. was born 1569, Maidstone, Kent County, England. He had three children, John, Jr., William and Katherine. John, Sr. was appointed "Keeper of the Goal" of Maidstone (Prison), Kent County, England, by King Charles I, of England in March 1631. This appointment is a "titled" position and is passed down from father to son. John, Sr. passed away in 1644 and the title "Keeper of the Goal" was passed to his son John Jr.

The first to come to the Colonies was William Collins, son of John Collins Sr. William, was born 1601, at age 34, set sail on the Plain Joane, which departed London on May 15, 1635, bound for Virginia. There was another William Collins, age 20, on board, believed to be William's nephew.

There is confusion over how many William Collins's there were in Virginia. The records cross each other with different wives and children, another example of naming them the same from generation to generation. Unraveling all the John Collins will be a challenge to sort out and a lifelong pursuit. My biological ancestry turns out to be Scotch-Irish and English on my father's side, which has a long history.

20. JOJO'S SEARCH

JoJo is still searching for her biological father, but her search has been a lot more difficult because her father is of Spanish ancestry. Our mother being of Spanish ancestry makes it difficult for JoJo because a lot of the surnames are similar. The difference in JoJo and me was that my biological father was not Spanish, so I could eliminate the Spanish surnames in my search for my paternal line. JoJo has also had many up and downs in her research. She thought she found, a half-brother, but after testing, it turned out to be false. She has no one person on any of the DNA sites that shows a high percentage of shared DNA. We are going by what our mother told her but wonder if it is accurate. After discovering that what my mother told me was not true, how can we trust what she told JoJo? She is still searching, and hopefully her story will have a happy ending and give her closure. I am currently helping in her research and research of other people and relatives I have found along my journey.

21. SUMMARY

In communicating with many genealogists about my story, they have indicated that it is a very interesting story of discovery and how DNA helped me find my family without a surname. I decided that it was worth telling, and all the twists and turns and different paths and disappointments and people I met along the way only makes my story more interesting. The only regret that I have is I wish I had not wasted so many years on the Casper and Cosper surname as my mother told me and had just concentrated on the DNA results and went that route. Of course it wouldn't make my story as interesting as it is.

Hopefully my story can help you if you are searching for your biological family. You, too, can find your roots whether you are adopted, are illegitimate, or have just been told the wrong information—you can find the truth and have closure. I am sure a lot of luck was also on my side in making my story a success, and I am truly appreciative of all the help from so many people and sources. I look forward to getting to know my new family and their history and hopefully making our relationship a lifelong one.

Made in the USA
Lexington, KY
09 May 2014